Cutting Expenses
A 52 Week Journal

Name _____

Phone _____

Email _____

Saving on expenses is a challenge. It's difficult to know where to begin and even see if it is working over time.

This journal is a 52-week plan to cut expenses, pinch pennies and save money.

Each week select one expense to cut and choose a substitute/replacement that costs less or is free. Be creative!

The best place to start is to look at bank statements and credit card bills. Knowing where the money is going, helps make choices on how where expenses can be cut. Subscriptions, going out to eat, specialty coffee drinks, and renegotiating interest rates or monthly bills like cable, internet or phone are popular places to begin.

Every expense cut is great success, whether the savings is $1 a month or $100 a year. At the end of 52 weeks, the overall savings are significant.

No one knows you better than yourself and which costs are negotiable, however the ideas are endless! You can do this!

Set a goal

How much money do you want to save by the end of 52 weeks? Why? Write a note below describing a goal dollar amount to save at the end of 52 weeks and what you will do with the saved money.

_____

_____

_____

_____

_____

Ideas for expenses to cut in the upcoming weeks

_____

_____   _____

_____   _____

_____   _____

_____   _____

_____   _____

_____   _____

_____   _____

_____   _____

_____   _____

_____   _____

_____   _____

_____   _____

_____   _____

Week 1

Date _____

Cut this expense: ✂ _____

_____

Substitute with: _____

_____

Cost of cut expense $ _____ per week/month/year (circle)

subtract -

Cost of replacement $ _____ per week/month/year (circle)

equals =

Expected savings $ _____ per week/month/year (circle)

Reflect on this choice in two months

On a scale of 1 to 5, how easy was it to stick to this plan? _____
(1 = very difficult. 5 = easy)

In reality, how much money have you saved since you made this choice?

$ _____ over _____ weeks/months (circle)

Week 2

Date _____

Cut this expense: ✂ _____

_____

Substitute with: _____

_____

Cost of cut expense $ _____ per week/month/year (circle)

subtract -

Cost of replacement $ _____ per week/month/year (circle)

equals =

Expected savings $ _____ per week/month/year (circle)

Reflect on this choice in two months

On a scale of 1 to 5, how easy was it to stick to this plan? _____
(1 = very difficult. 5 = easy)

In reality, how much money have you saved since you made this choice?

$ _____ over _____ weeks/months (circle)

Week 3

Date _____

Cut this expense: ✂ _____

_____

Substitute with: _____

_____

Cost of cut expense $ _____ per week/month/year (circle)

subtract **-**

Cost of replacement $ _____ per week/month/year (circle)

equals **=**

Expected savings $ _____ per week/month/year (circle)

Reflect on this choice in two months

On a scale of 1 to 5, how easy was it to stick to this plan? _____
(1 = very difficult. 5 = easy)

In reality, how much money have you saved since you made this choice?

$ _____ over _____ weeks/months (circle)

Week 4

Date _____

Cut this expense: ✂ _____

_____

Substitute with: _____

_____

Cost of cut expense $ _____ per week/month/year (circle)

subtract **-**

Cost of replacement $ _____ per week/month/year (circle)

equals **=**

Expected savings $ _____ per week/month/year (circle)

Reflect on this choice in two months

On a scale of 1 to 5, how easy was it to stick to this plan? _____
(1 = very difficult. 5 = easy)

In reality, how much money have you saved since you made this choice?

$ _____ over _____ weeks/months (circle)

Week 5

Date _____

Cut this expense: ✂————————————————————

_____

Substitute with: _____

_____

Cost of cut expense $ _____ per week/month/year (circle)

subtract −

Cost of replacement $ _____ per week/month/year (circle)

equals =

Expected savings $ _____ per week/month/year (circle)

Reflect on this choice in two months

On a scale of 1 to 5, how easy was it to stick to this plan? _____
(1 = very difficult. 5 = easy)

In reality, how much money have you saved since you made this choice?

$ _____ over _____ weeks/months (circle)

Week 6

Date _____

Cut this expense: ✂ _____

_____

Substitute with: _____

_____

Cost of cut expense $ _____ per week/month/year (circle)

subtract **-**

Cost of replacement $ _____ per week/month/year (circle)

equals **=**

Expected savings $ _____ per week/month/year (circle)

Reflect on this choice in two months

On a scale of 1 to 5, how easy was it to stick to this plan? _____
(1 = very difficult. 5 = easy)

In reality, how much money have you saved since you made this choice?

$ _____ over _____ weeks/months (circle)

Week 7

Date _____

Cut this expense: ✂ _____

_____

Substitute with: _____

_____

_____

Cost of cut expense $ _____ per week/month/year (circle)

subtract **-**

Cost of replacement $ _____ per week/month/year (circle)

equals **=**

Expected savings $ _____ per week/month/year (circle)

Reflect on this choice in two months

On a scale of 1 to 5, how easy was it to stick to this plan? _____
(1 = very difficult. 5 = easy)

In reality, how much money have you saved since you made this choice?

$ _____ over _____ weeks/months (circle)

Week 8

Date _____

Cut this expense: ✂ _____

_____

Substitute with: _____

_____

Cost of cut expense $ _____ per week/month/year (circle)

subtract **-**

Cost of replacement $ _____ per week/month/year (circle)

equals **=**

Expected savings $ _____ per week/month/year (circle)

Reflect on this choice in two months

On a scale of 1 to 5, how easy was it to stick to this plan? _____
(1 = very difficult. 5 = easy)

In reality, how much money have you saved since you made this choice?

$ _____ over _____ weeks/months (circle)

Week 9

Date _____

Cut this expense: ✂ _____

_____

Substitute with: _____

_____

Cost of cut expense $ _____ per week/month/year (circle)

subtract -

Cost of replacement $ _____ per week/month/year (circle)

equals =

Expected savings $ _____ per week/month/year (circle)

Reflect on this choice in two months

On a scale of 1 to 5, how easy was it to stick to this plan? _____
(1 = very difficult. 5 = easy)

In reality, how much money have you saved since you made this choice?

$ _____ over _____ weeks/months (circle)

Week 10

Date _____

Cut this expense: ✂ _____

_____

Substitute with: _____

_____

Cost of cut expense $ _____ per week/month/year (circle)

subtract -

Cost of replacement $ _____ per week/month/year (circle)

equals =

Expected savings $ _____ per week/month/year (circle)

Reflect on this choice in two months

On a scale of 1 to 5, how easy was it to stick to this plan? _____
(1 = very difficult. 5 = easy)

In reality, how much money have you saved since you made this choice?

$ _____ over _____ weeks/months (circle)

Week 11

Date _____

Cut this expense: ✂ _____

_____

Substitute with: _____

_____

Cost of cut expense $ _____ per week/month/year (circle)

subtract -

Cost of replacement $ _____ per week/month/year (circle)

equals =

Expected savings $ _____ per week/month/year (circle)

Reflect on this choice in two months

On a scale of 1 to 5, how easy was it to stick to this plan? _____
(1 = very difficult. 5 = easy)

In reality, how much money have you saved since you made this choice?

$ _____ over _____ weeks/months (circle)

Week 12

Date _____

Cut this expense: ✂ _____

_____

Substitute with: _____

_____

Cost of cut expense $ _____ per week/month/year (circle)

subtract -

Cost of replacement $ _____ per week/month/year (circle)

equals =

Expected savings $ _____ per week/month/year (circle)

Reflect on this choice in two months

On a scale of 1 to 5, how easy was it to stick to this plan? _____
(1 = very difficult. 5 = easy)

In reality, how much money have you saved since you made this choice?

$ _____ over _____ weeks/months (circle)

Week 13

Date _____

Cut this expense: ✂ _____

_____

Substitute with: _____

_____

Cost of cut expense $ _____ per week/month/year (circle)

subtract **-**

Cost of replacement $ _____ per week/month/year (circle)

equals **=**

Expected savings $ _____ per week/month/year (circle)

Reflect on this choice in two months

On a scale of 1 to 5, how easy was it to stick to this plan? _____
(1 = very difficult. 5 = easy)

In reality, how much money have you saved since you made this choice?

$ _____ over _____ weeks/months (circle)

Week 14

Date _____

Cut this expense: ✄ _____

_____

Substitute with: _____

_____

Cost of cut expense $ _____ per week/month/year (circle)

subtract -

Cost of replacement $ _____ per week/month/year (circle)

equals =

Expected savings $ _____ per week/month/year (circle)

Reflect on this choice in two months

On a scale of 1 to 5, how easy was it to stick to this plan? _____
(1 = very difficult. 5 = easy)

In reality, how much money have you saved since you made this choice?

$ _____ over _____ weeks/months (circle)

Week 15

Date _____

Cut this expense: ✂ _____

_____

Substitute with: _____

_____

_____

Cost of cut expense $ _____ per week/month/year (circle)

subtract -

Cost of replacement $ _____ per week/month/year (circle)

equals =

Expected savings $ _____ per week/month/year (circle)

Reflect on this choice in two months

On a scale of 1 to 5, how easy was it to stick to this plan? _____
(1 = very difficult. 5 = easy)

In reality, how much money have you saved since you made this choice?

$ _____ over _____ weeks/months (circle)

Week 16

Date _____

Cut this expense: ✂ _____

_____

Substitute with: _____

_____

Cost of cut expense $ _____ per week/month/year (circle)

subtract -

Cost of replacement $ _____ per week/month/year (circle)

equals =

Expected savings $ _____ per week/month/year (circle)

Reflect on this choice in two months

On a scale of 1 to 5, how easy was it to stick to this plan? _____
(1 = very difficult. 5 = easy)

In reality, how much money have you saved since you made this choice?

$ _____ over _____ weeks/months (circle)

Week 17

Date _____

Cut this expense: ✂ _____

_____

Substitute with: _____

_____

Cost of cut expense $ _____ per week/month/year (circle)

subtract -

Cost of replacement $ _____ per week/month/year (circle)

equals =

Expected savings $ _____ per week/month/year (circle)

Reflect on this choice in two months

On a scale of 1 to 5, how easy was it to stick to this plan? _____
(1 = very difficult. 5 = easy)

In reality, how much money have you saved since you made this choice?

$ _____ over _____ weeks/months (circle)

Week 18

Date   _____

Cut this expense: ✂ _____

_____

Substitute with: _____

_____

Cost of cut expense $ _____   per week/month/year (circle)

         subtract   -

Cost of replacement $ _____   per week/month/year (circle)

          equals   =

Expected savings $ _____   per week/month/year (circle)

Reflect on this choice in two months

On a scale of 1 to 5, how easy was it to stick to this plan? _____
(1 = very difficult. 5 = easy)

In reality, how much money have you saved since you made this choice?

$ _____ over _____ weeks/months (circle)

Week 19

Date _____

Cut this expense: ✂ _____

_____

Substitute with: _____

_____

_____

Cost of cut expense $ _____ per week/month/year (circle)

subtract −

Cost of replacement $ _____ per week/month/year (circle)

equals =

Expected savings $ _____ per week/month/year (circle)

Reflect on this choice in two months

On a scale of 1 to 5, how easy was it to stick to this plan? _____
(1 = very difficult. 5 = easy)

In reality, how much money have you saved since you made this choice?

$ _____ over _____ weeks/months (circle)

Week 20

Date _____

Cut this expense: ✂ _____

_____

Substitute with: _____

_____

Cost of cut expense $ _____ per week/month/year (circle)

subtract -

Cost of replacement $ _____ per week/month/year (circle)

equals =

Expected savings $ _____ per week/month/year (circle)

Reflect on this choice in two months

On a scale of 1 to 5, how easy was it to stick to this plan? _____
(1 = very difficult. 5 = easy)

In reality, how much money have you saved since you made this choice?

$ _____ over _____ weeks/months (circle)

Week 21

Date _____

Cut this expense: ✂ _____

_____

Substitute with: _____

_____

Cost of cut expense $ _____ per week/month/year (circle)

subtract -

Cost of replacement $ _____ per week/month/year (circle)

equals =

Expected savings $ _____ per week/month/year (circle)

Reflect on this choice in two months

On a scale of 1 to 5, how easy was it to stick to this plan? _____
(1 = very difficult. 5 = easy)

In reality, how much money have you saved since you made this choice?

$ _____ over _____ weeks/months (circle)

Week 22

Date _____

Cut this expense: ✂ _____

_____

Substitute with: _____

_____

Cost of cut expense $ _____ per week/month/year (circle)

subtract -

Cost of replacement $ _____ per week/month/year (circle)

equals =

Expected savings $ _____ per week/month/year (circle)

Reflect on this choice in two months

On a scale of 1 to 5, how easy was it to stick to this plan? _____
(1 = very difficult. 5 = easy)

In reality, how much money have you saved since you made this choice?

$ _____ over _____ weeks/months (circle)

Week 23

Date _____

Cut this expense: ✂ _____

_____

Substitute with: _____

_____

Cost of cut expense $ _____ per week/month/year (circle)

subtract **-**

Cost of replacement $ _____ per week/month/year (circle)

equals **=**

Expected savings $ _____ per week/month/year (circle)

Reflect on this choice in two months

On a scale of 1 to 5, how easy was it to stick to this plan? _____
(1 = very difficult. 5 = easy)

In reality, how much money have you saved since you made this choice?

$ _____ over _____ weeks/months (circle)

Week 24

Date _____

Cut this expense: ✂ _____

_____

Substitute with: _____

_____

Cost of cut expense $ _____ per week/month/year (circle)

subtract **-**

Cost of replacement $ _____ per week/month/year (circle)

equals **=**

Expected savings $ _____ per week/month/year (circle)

Reflect on this choice in two months

On a scale of 1 to 5, how easy was it to stick to this plan? _____
(1 = very difficult. 5 = easy)

In reality, how much money have you saved since you made this choice?

$ _____ over _____ weeks/months (circle)

Week 25

Date _____

Cut this expense: ✂ _____

_____

Substitute with: _____

_____

Cost of cut expense $ _____ per week/month/year (circle)

subtract −

Cost of replacement $ _____ per week/month/year (circle)

equals =

Expected savings $ _____ per week/month/year (circle)

Reflect on this choice in two months

On a scale of 1 to 5, how easy was it to stick to this plan? _____
(1 = very difficult. 5 = easy)

In reality, how much money have you saved since you made this choice?

$ _____ over _____ weeks/months (circle)

Week 26

Date _____

Cut this expense: ✂ _____

_____

Substitute with: _____

_____

Cost of cut expense $ _____ per week/month/year (circle)

subtract -

Cost of replacement $ _____ per week/month/year (circle)

equals =

Expected savings $ _____ per week/month/year (circle)

Reflect on this choice in two months

On a scale of 1 to 5, how easy was it to stick to this plan? _____
(1 = very difficult. 5 = easy)

In reality, how much money have you saved since you made this choice?

$ _____ over _____ weeks/months (circle)

Week 27

Date _____

Cut this expense: ✂ _____

_____

Substitute with: _____

_____

Cost of cut expense $ _____ per week/month/year (circle)

  subtract -

Cost of replacement $ _____ per week/month/year (circle)

  equals =

Expected savings $ _____ per week/month/year (circle)

Reflect on this choice in two months

On a scale of 1 to 5, how easy was it to stick to this plan? _____
(1 = very difficult. 5 = easy)

In reality, how much money have you saved since you made this choice?

$ _____ over _____ weeks/months (circle)

Week 28

Date _____

Cut this expense: ✂ _____

_____

Substitute with: _____

_____

Cost of cut expense $ _____ per week/month/year (circle)

subtract -

Cost of replacement $ _____ per week/month/year (circle)

equals =

Expected savings $ _____ per week/month/year (circle)

Reflect on this choice in two months

On a scale of 1 to 5, how easy was it to stick to this plan? _____
(1 = very difficult. 5 = easy)

In reality, how much money have you saved since you made this choice?

$ _____ over _____ weeks/months (circle)

Week 29

Date _____

Cut this expense: ✂ _____

_____

Substitute with: _____

_____

Cost of cut expense $ _____ per week/month/year (circle)

subtract -

Cost of replacement $ _____ per week/month/year (circle)

equals =

Expected savings $ _____ per week/month/year (circle)

Reflect on this choice in two months

On a scale of 1 to 5, how easy was it to stick to this plan? _____
(1 = very difficult. 5 = easy)

In reality, how much money have you saved since you made this choice?

$ _____ over _____ weeks/months (circle)

Week 30

Date _____

Cut this expense: ✂ _____

_____

Substitute with: _____

_____

Cost of cut expense $ _____ per week/month/year (circle)

subtract -

Cost of replacement $ _____ per week/month/year (circle)

equals =

Expected savings $ _____ per week/month/year (circle)

Reflect on this choice in two months

On a scale of 1 to 5, how easy was it to stick to this plan? _____
(1 = very difficult. 5 = easy)

In reality, how much money have you saved since you made this choice?

$ _____ over _____ weeks/months (circle)

Week 31

Date _____

Cut this expense: ✂ _____

_____

Substitute with: _____

_____

Cost of cut expense $ _____ per week/month/year (circle)

subtract -

Cost of replacement $ _____ per week/month/year (circle)

equals =

Expected savings $ _____ per week/month/year (circle)

Reflect on this choice in two months

On a scale of 1 to 5, how easy was it to stick to this plan? _____
(1 = very difficult. 5 = easy)

In reality, how much money have you saved since you made this choice?

$ _____ over _____ weeks/months (circle)

Week 32

Date _____

Cut this expense: ✂ _____

_____

Substitute with: _____

_____

Cost of cut expense $ _____ per week/month/year (circle)

subtract -

Cost of replacement $ _____ per week/month/year (circle)

equals =

Expected savings $ _____ per week/month/year (circle)

Reflect on this choice in two months

On a scale of 1 to 5, how easy was it to stick to this plan? _____
(1 = very difficult. 5 = easy)

In reality, how much money have you saved since you made this choice?

$ _____ over _____ weeks/months (circle)

Week 33

Date _____

Cut this expense: ✂ _____

_____

Substitute with: _____

_____

Cost of cut expense $ _____ per week/month/year (circle)

subtract **-**

Cost of replacement $ _____ per week/month/year (circle)

equals **=**

Expected savings $ _____ per week/month/year (circle)

Reflect on this choice in two months

On a scale of 1 to 5, how easy was it to stick to this plan? _____
(1 = very difficult. 5 = easy)

In reality, how much money have you saved since you made this choice?

$ _____ over _____ weeks/months (circle)

Week 34

Date _____

Cut this expense: ✂ _____

_____

Substitute with: _____

_____

Cost of cut expense $ _____ per week/month/year (circle)

subtract −

Cost of replacement $ _____ per week/month/year (circle)

equals =

Expected savings $ _____ per week/month/year (circle)

Reflect on this choice in two months

On a scale of 1 to 5, how easy was it to stick to this plan? _____
(1 = very difficult. 5 = easy)

In reality, how much money have you saved since you made this choice?

$ _____ over _____ weeks/months (circle)

Week 35

Date _____

Cut this expense: ✂ _____

_____

Substitute with: _____

_____

Cost of cut expense $ _____ per week/month/year (circle)

subtract -

Cost of replacement $ _____ per week/month/year (circle)

equals =

Expected savings $ _____ per week/month/year (circle)

Reflect on this choice in two months

On a scale of 1 to 5, how easy was it to stick to this plan? _____
(1 = very difficult. 5 = easy)

In reality, how much money have you saved since you made this choice?

$ _____ over _____ weeks/months (circle)

Week 36

Date _____

Cut this expense: ✂ _____

_____

Substitute with: _____

_____

Cost of cut expense $ _____ per week/month/year (circle)

subtract **-**

Cost of replacement $ _____ per week/month/year (circle)

equals **=**

Expected savings $ _____ per week/month/year (circle)

Reflect on this choice in two months

On a scale of 1 to 5, how easy was it to stick to this plan? _____
(1 = very difficult. 5 = easy)

In reality, how much money have you saved since you made this choice?

$ _____ over _____ weeks/months (circle)

Week 37

Date _____

Cut this expense: ✂ _____

_____

Substitute with: _____

_____

Cost of cut expense $ _____ per week/month/year (circle)

subtract -

Cost of replacement $ _____ per week/month/year (circle)

equals =

Expected savings $ _____ per week/month/year (circle)

Reflect on this choice in two months

On a scale of 1 to 5, how easy was it to stick to this plan? _____
(1 = very difficult. 5 = easy)

In reality, how much money have you saved since you made this choice?

$ _____ over _____ weeks/months (circle)

Week 38

Date _____

Cut this expense: ✂ _____

_____

Substitute with: _____

_____

Cost of cut expense $ _____ per week/month/year (circle)

subtract -

Cost of replacement $ _____ per week/month/year (circle)

equals =

Expected savings $ _____ per week/month/year (circle)

Reflect on this choice in two months

On a scale of 1 to 5, how easy was it to stick to this plan? _____
(1 = very difficult. 5 = easy)

In reality, how much money have you saved since you made this choice?

$ _____ over _____ weeks/months (circle)

Week 39

Date _____

Cut this expense: ✂ _____

_____

Substitute with: _____

_____

Cost of cut expense $ _____ per week/month/year (circle)

subtract -

Cost of replacement $ _____ per week/month/year (circle)

equals =

Expected savings $ _____ per week/month/year (circle)

Reflect on this choice in two months

On a scale of 1 to 5, how easy was it to stick to this plan? _____
(1 = very difficult. 5 = easy)

In reality, how much money have you saved since you made this choice?

$ _____ over _____ weeks/months (circle)

Week 40

Date _____

Cut this expense: ✂ _____

_____

Substitute with: _____

_____

Cost of cut expense $ _____ per week/month/year (circle)

subtract **-**

Cost of replacement $ _____ per week/month/year (circle)

equals **=**

Expected savings $ _____ per week/month/year (circle)

Reflect on this choice in two months

On a scale of 1 to 5, how easy was it to stick to this plan? _____
(1 = very difficult. 5 = easy)

In reality, how much money have you saved since you made this choice?

$ _____ over _____ weeks/months (circle)

Week 41

Date _____

Cut this expense: ✄ _____

_____

Substitute with: _____

_____

Cost of cut expense $ _____ per week/month/year (circle)

subtract -

Cost of replacement $ _____ per week/month/year (circle)

equals =

Expected savings $ _____ per week/month/year (circle)

Reflect on this choice in two months

On a scale of 1 to 5, how easy was it to stick to this plan? _____
(1 = very difficult. 5 = easy)

In reality, how much money have you saved since you made this choice?

$ _____ over _____ weeks/months (circle)

Week 42

Date _____

Cut this expense: ✂ _____

_____

Substitute with: _____

_____

Cost of cut expense $ _____ per week/month/year (circle)

subtract -

Cost of replacement $ _____ per week/month/year (circle)

equals =

Expected savings $ _____ per week/month/year (circle)

Reflect on this choice in two months

On a scale of 1 to 5, how easy was it to stick to this plan? _____
(1 = very difficult. 5 = easy)

In reality, how much money have you saved since you made this choice?

$ _____ over _____ weeks/months (circle)

Week 43

Date _____

Cut this expense: ✂ _____

_____

Substitute with: _____

_____

Cost of cut expense $ _____ per week/month/year (circle)

subtract **-**

Cost of replacement $ _____ per week/month/year (circle)

equals **=**

Expected savings $ _____ per week/month/year (circle)

Reflect on this choice in two months

On a scale of 1 to 5, how easy was it to stick to this plan? _____
(1 = very difficult. 5 = easy)

In reality, how much money have you saved since you made this choice?

$ _____ over _____ weeks/months (circle)

Week 44

Date _____

Cut this expense: ✂ _____

_____

Substitute with: _____

_____

Cost of cut expense $ _____ per week/month/year (circle)

subtract -

Cost of replacement $ _____ per week/month/year (circle)

equals =

Expected savings $ _____ per week/month/year (circle)

Reflect on this choice in two months

On a scale of 1 to 5, how easy was it to stick to this plan? _____
(1 = very difficult. 5 = easy)

In reality, how much money have you saved since you made this choice?

$ _____ over _____ weeks/months (circle)

Week 45

Date _____

Cut this expense: ✂ _____

_____

Substitute with: _____

_____

Cost of cut expense $ _____ per week/month/year (circle)

subtract -

Cost of replacement $ _____ per week/month/year (circle)

equals =

Expected savings $ _____ per week/month/year (circle)

Reflect on this choice in two months

On a scale of 1 to 5, how easy was it to stick to this plan? _____
(1 = very difficult. 5 = easy)

In reality, how much money have you saved since you made this choice?

$ _____ over _____ weeks/months (circle)

Week 46

Date _____

Cut this expense: ✂ _____

_____

Substitute with: _____

_____

Cost of cut expense $ _____ per week/month/year (circle)

subtract -

Cost of replacement $ _____ per week/month/year (circle)

equals =

Expected savings $ _____ per week/month/year (circle)

Reflect on this choice in two months

On a scale of 1 to 5, how easy was it to stick to this plan? _____
(1 = very difficult. 5 = easy)

In reality, how much money have you saved since you made this choice?

$ _____ over _____ weeks/months (circle)

Week 47

Date _____

Cut this expense: ✂ _____

_____

Substitute with: _____

_____

Cost of cut expense $ _____ per week/month/year (circle)

subtract **-**

Cost of replacement $ _____ per week/month/year (circle)

equals **=**

Expected savings $ _____ per week/month/year (circle)

Reflect on this choice in two months

On a scale of 1 to 5, how easy was it to stick to this plan? _____
(1 = very difficult. 5 = easy)

In reality, how much money have you saved since you made this choice?

$ _____ over _____ weeks/months (circle)

Week 48

Date _____

Cut this expense: ✂ _____

_____

Substitute with: _____

_____

Cost of cut expense $ _____ per week/month/year (circle)

subtract -

Cost of replacement $ _____ per week/month/year (circle)

equals =

Expected savings $ _____ per week/month/year (circle)

Reflect on this choice in two months

On a scale of 1 to 5, how easy was it to stick to this plan? _____
(1 = very difficult. 5 = easy)

In reality, how much money have you saved since you made this choice?

$ _____ over _____ weeks/months (circle)

Week 49

Date _____

Cut this expense: ✂ _____

_____

Substitute with: _____

_____

_____

Cost of cut expense $ _____ per week/month/year (circle)

subtract **-**

Cost of replacement $ _____ per week/month/year (circle)

equals **=**

Expected savings $ _____ per week/month/year (circle)

Reflect on this choice in two months

On a scale of 1 to 5, how easy was it to stick to this plan? _____
(1 = very difficult. 5 = easy)

In reality, how much money have you saved since you made this choice?

$ _____ over _____ weeks/months (circle)

Week 50

Date _____

Cut this expense: ✂ _____

_____

Substitute with: _____

_____

Cost of cut expense $ _____ per week/month/year (circle)

subtract **-**

Cost of replacement $ _____ per week/month/year (circle)

equals **=**

Expected savings $ _____ per week/month/year (circle)

Reflect on this choice in two months

On a scale of 1 to 5, how easy was it to stick to this plan? _____
(1 = very difficult. 5 = easy)

In reality, how much money have you saved since you made this choice?

$ _____ over _____ weeks/months (circle)

Week 51

Date _____

Cut this expense: ✂ _____

_____

Substitute with: _____

_____

Cost of cut expense $ _____ per week/month/year (circle)

subtract -

Cost of replacement $ _____ per week/month/year (circle)

equals =

Expected savings $ _____ per week/month/year (circle)

Reflect on this choice in two months

On a scale of 1 to 5, how easy was it to stick to this plan? _____
(1 = very difficult. 5 = easy)

In reality, how much money have you saved since you made this choice?

$ _____ over _____ weeks/months (circle)

Week 52

Date _____

Cut this expense: ✂ _____

_____

Substitute with: _____

_____

Cost of cut expense $ _____ per week/month/year (circle)

subtract -

Cost of replacement $ _____ per week/month/year (circle)

equals =

Expected savings $ _____ per week/month/year (circle)

Reflect on this choice in two months

On a scale of 1 to 5, how easy was it to stick to this plan? _____
(1 = very difficult. 5 = easy)

In reality, how much money have you saved since you made this choice?

$ _____ over _____ weeks/months (circle)

Congratulations! You found a way to save money 52 times! Let's see how your savings added up. Add the savings from each week to calculate the total savings you've achieved.

NOTE: Be consistent with the weekly savings values. Consider inputting each week's savings as an annual amount. Multiply weekly savings by 52 or monthly savings by 12 to calculate annual savings.

Week 1 _____	Week 20 _____	Week 40 _____
Week 2 _____	Week 21 _____	Week 41 _____
Week 3 _____	Week 22 _____	Week 42 _____
Week 4 _____	Week 23 _____	Week 43 _____
Week 5 _____	Week 24 _____	Week 44 _____
Week 6 _____	Week 25 _____	Week 45 _____
Week 7 _____	Week 26 _____	Week 46 _____
Week 8 _____	Week 27 _____	Week 47 _____
Week 9 _____	Week 28 _____	Week 48 _____
Week 10 _____	Week 29 _____	Week 49 _____
Week 11 _____	Week 30 _____	Week 50 _____
Week 12 _____	Week 32 _____	Week 51 _____
Week 13 _____	Week 33 _____	Week 52 _____
Week 14 _____	Week 34 _____	
Week 15 _____	Week 35 _____	**Total Savings:** _____
Week 16 _____	Week 36 _____	
Week 17 _____	Week 37 _____	**Did you meet your goal?**
Week 18 _____	Week 38 _____	❑ Yes!
Week 19 _____	Week 39 _____	❑ Almost! Need a few more weeks.